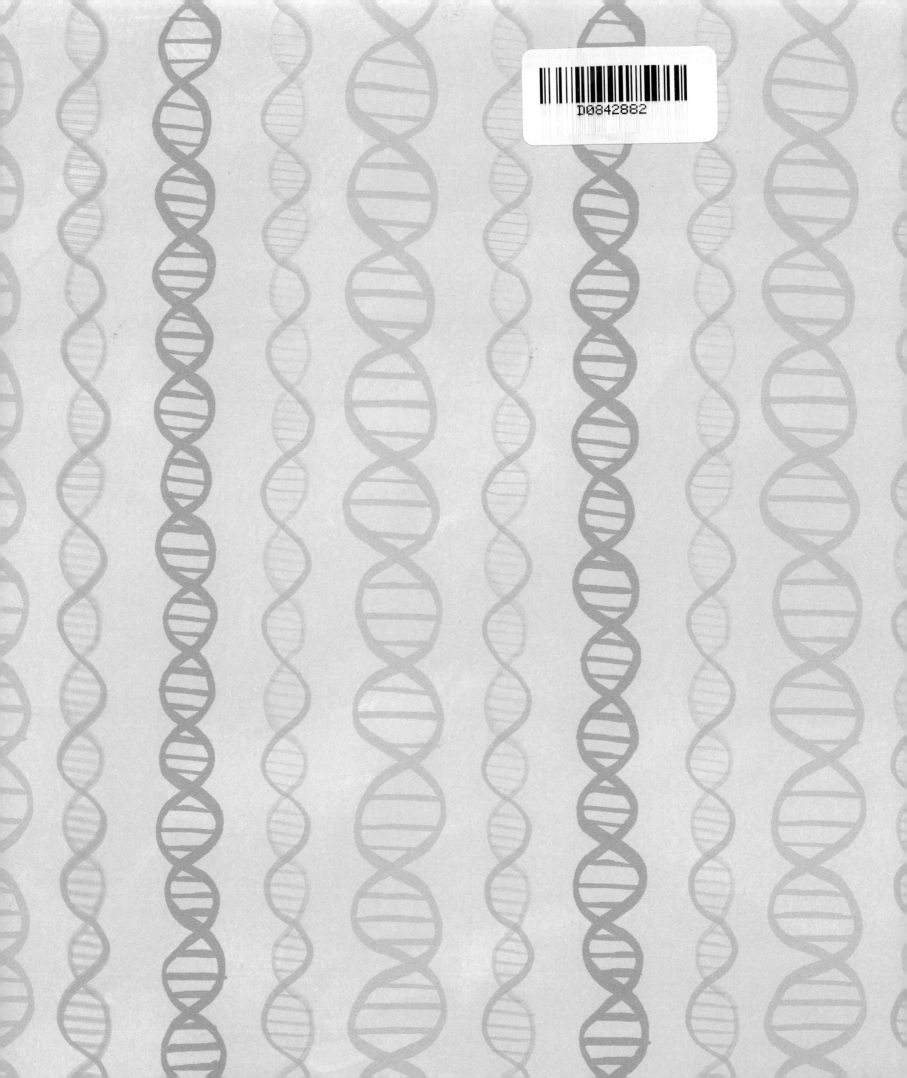

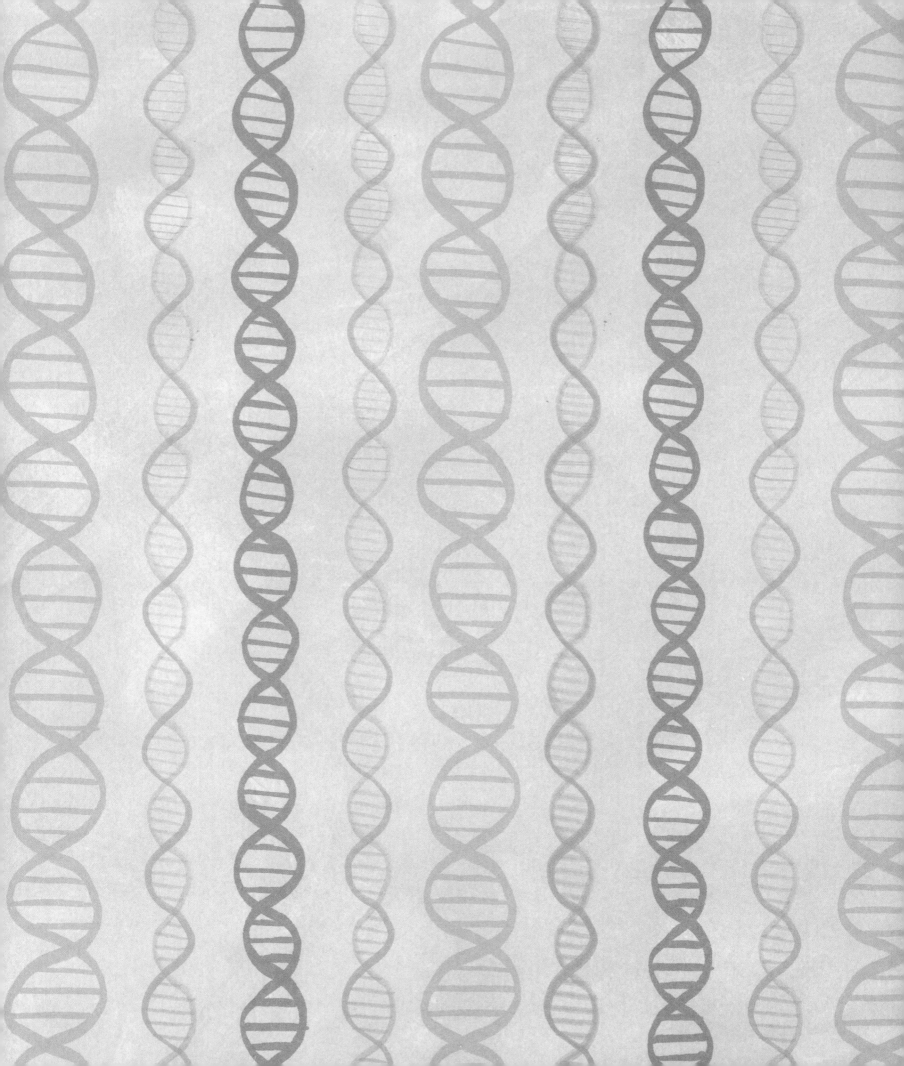

The One and Only Me

Copyright © 2016 by Ariana Killoran
and 23andMe, Inc.

Book design by *Ariana Killoran*
and *Iain R. Morris*
Design assistance by *Melissa N. Greenberg*
Edited by *Amy Novesky*
Content and editorial assistance from
Alison Chubb, Ashley Horgan, Esther Kim
and *Joanna Mountain* of 23andMe

Book design and packaging by:
CAMERON + COMPANY
www.cameronbooks.com

23andMe®

www.23andme.com

Library of Congress Control
Number available

ISBN: 978-0-9891537-1-3

10 9 8 7 6 5 4 3 2

Printed in the United States

the ONE and ONLY ME

A Book About GENES

ARIANA KILLORAN

A 23andMe Book

These are my parents.

milo   Cece

And these two are my brother and sister. Everyone says they look a lot alike.

WHY DO I LOOK SO DIFFERENT?

You look the way you do because of your genes!

JEANS? I love jeans!! I have seven pairs.

Genes are the instructions for making you. Your genes are everywhere in your body. They are very tiny, so you need a microscope to see them. They are inside your cells.

brain cells

skin cells

heart cells

You are made of trillions of cells: brain cells, hair cells, heart cells, and many more. And almost every cell has a complete set of your genes inside.

If you zoomed in on a single skin cell, you would see this:

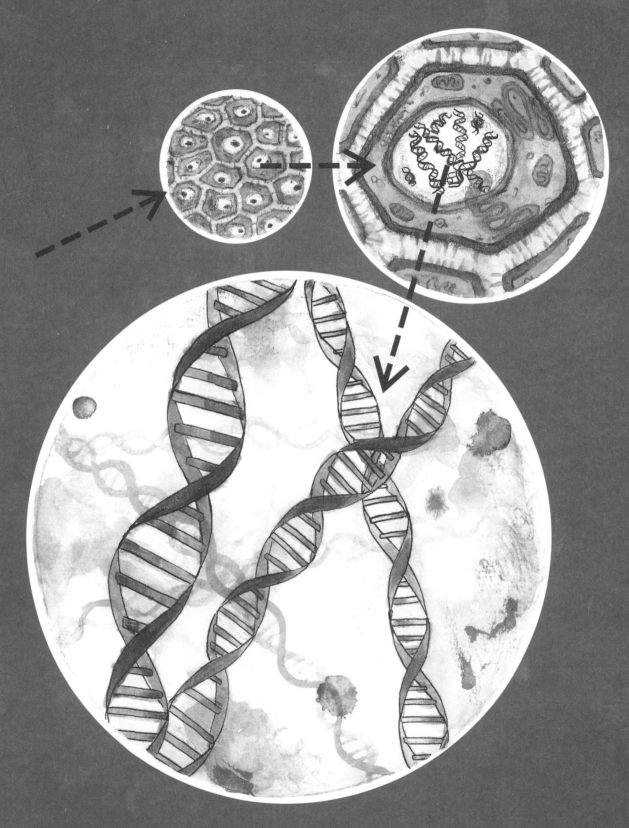

Your genes are right there in the middle of each cell. They are made of DNA, a long spiraling molecule found in all living creatures.

Genes tell your cells what types of cells to be

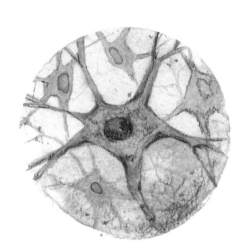

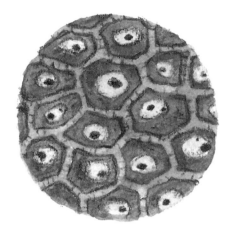

be a
brain
cell

be a
heart
cell

be a
skin cell

and what jobs to do,

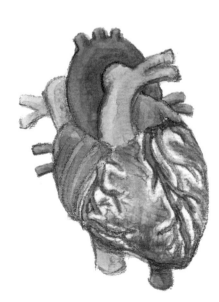

pump blood, heart!

Hey skin,
protect
the body!

make it curly

be blue

be freckly

and make you look the way you do.

You inherited your genes (all 20,000 of them!) from your parents. You have two versions of each gene—one from Mom and one from Dad. These two versions may be the same or a little bit different.

But WHICH version makes me look the way I do? WHO DECIDES? Or do they work TOGETHER?

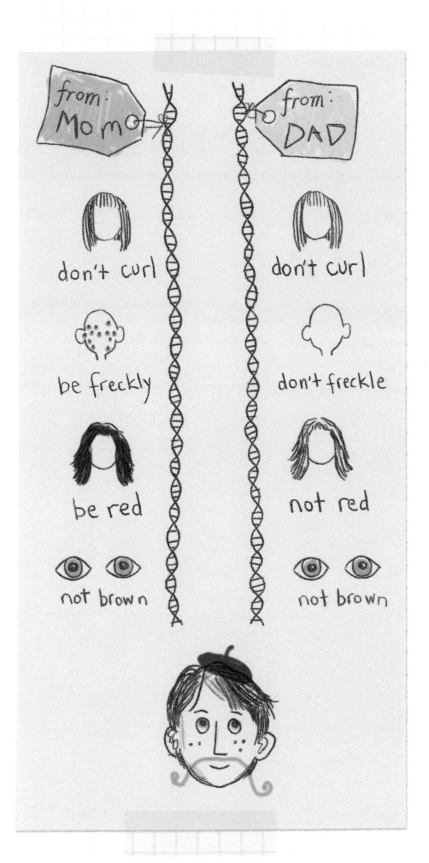

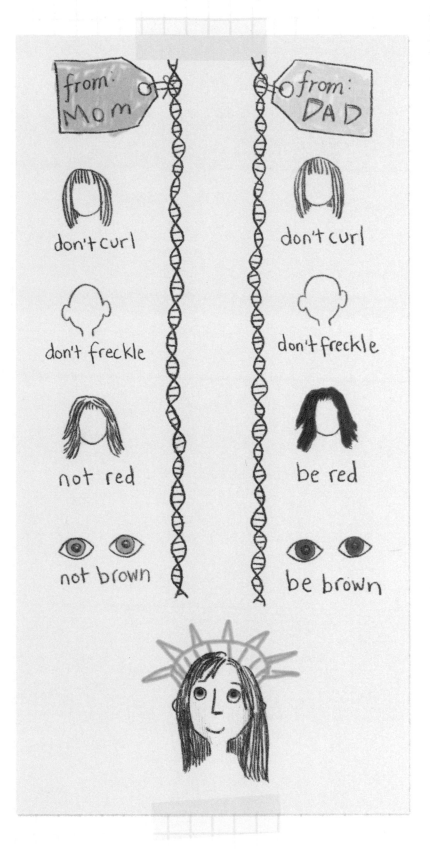

Your siblings also got two versions of every gene from your parents.
Some of them are exactly the same as the ones you inherited from
your parents, and some aren't.

In some cases, one version of a gene has a bigger effect than the other. For example, one important gene for eye color comes in either "brown" or "not brown." Because the brown version is stronger, you only need one "brown" version to have brown eyes.

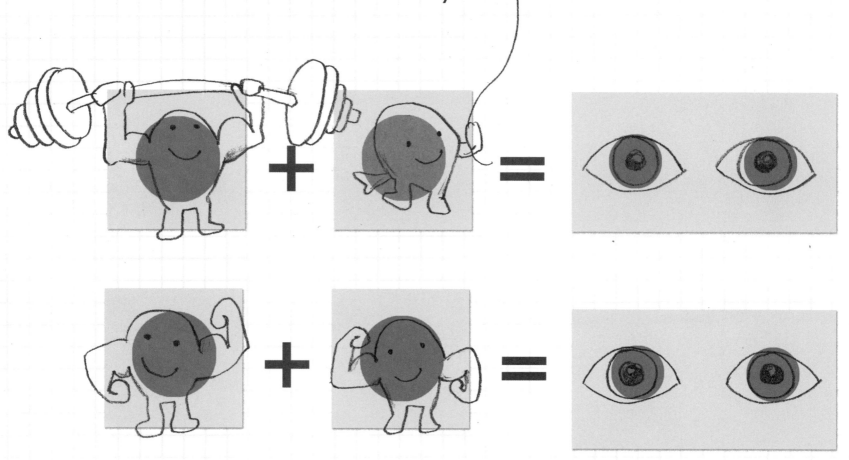

But it takes two "not brown" versions to give you blue, green, or something in between.

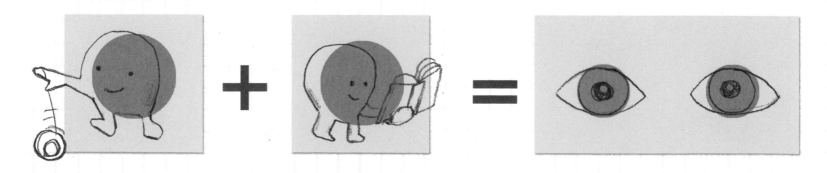

BUT WHERE DID I GET MY RED HAIR?

You can have red hair (or blue eyes) even if your parents don't. If your mom and dad each have one red version of a certain hair color gene, they won't have red hair themselves. But, if they both pass their red versions on to you, you probably will!

Your parents got their genes from their parents—your grandparents—
who got their genes from THEIR parents—your great-grandparents.
So you share genes with all these folks, too! Maybe there are some
other redheads in your family tree.

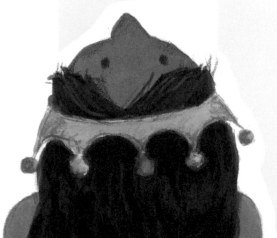

In fact, your genes have quite a history! They tell a story about all the people in your family who came before you, from all over the world, back through the ages. Who knows whose genes the three of you might share!

While single genes have big effects on your red hair and whether or not you have brown eyes, most characteristics about you are the result of many genes working together.

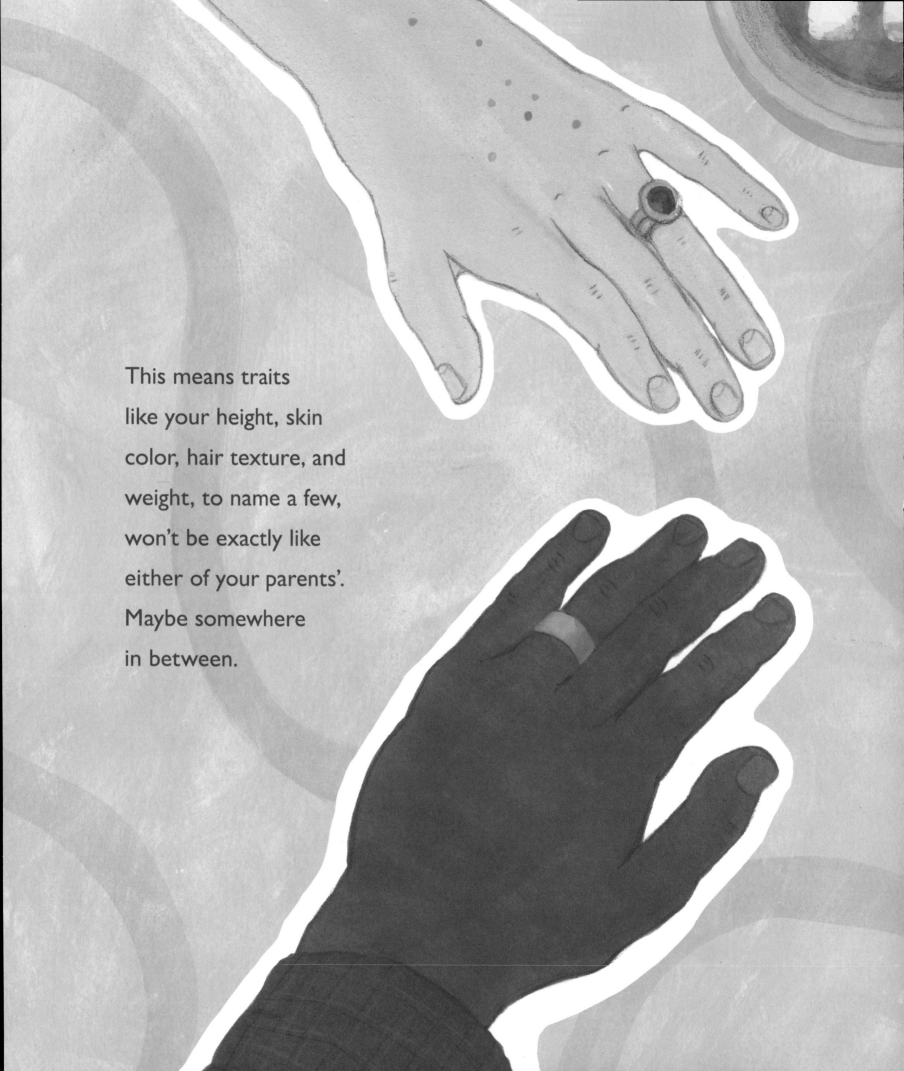

This means traits like your height, skin color, hair texture, and weight, to name a few, won't be exactly like either of your parents'. Maybe somewhere in between.

And genes are only a piece of what makes you who you are.
You are a mix of both your genes and the world around you:

the time you spent in
your mother's womb,

the foods you eat,

where you live,

the air you breathe,

the exercise you do,

the people you meet,

and the books you read.

All these work with your genes to make **the one and only you**.

DAD —— —

MOM —— —

milo ——————

For example, your height is determined mostly by your genes—hundreds, in fact! But what you eat and drink also affects your height.

Cece

Eggnog

Your genes affect your weight, too. But remember, what you eat and drink and how much you exercise are just as important.

While the color of your skin depends on many genes, a lot of sunlight can change the color of your skin, at least temporarily.

As for your personality,
well, we're just not sure.

Every day, scientists learn more about
how your genes shape who you are.

OK, so we all have GENES from our  and they tell our how to make us who we are. I have one version from MOM and one version from DAD.

So do my but not exactly the same versions I have. The little differences make us unique. Genes are very important for and but may be less important for whether or not I like making .

she does.

Because of my genes, I am both similar to and different from the rest of my family. My genes explain a lot about who I am. But as for who I become, that is up to me!

fun facts

Your DNA is **99.5%** identical to other people's DNA, and **96%** identical to the DNA of chimpanzees.

You and a mouse share **80%** of your genes.

You and a zebrafish share **63%** of your genes.

You and a fruit fly share **39%** of your genes.

If you stretched out the DNA from a single cell in your body, it would be about six feet long.

If you stretched out the DNA from ALL of the cells in your body, it could reach to the sun and back hundreds of times.

LEARN MORE ABOUT GENETICS

Genetics 101 at www.23andme.com/gen101

GLOSSARY

cell: Cells are the units that make up all the tissues in your body. Some examples are skin cells, brain cells, bone cells, and blood cells. Most cells contain a copy of all of our genes. The human body has about 37 trillion cells. ✿

gene: A gene is a sequence of DNA that contains an instruction for making a specific substance that your body uses to build itself and function. Humans have about 20,000 genes, each with an instruction for making something different. ✿

DNA: DNA is a long, spiraling molecule that stores the instructions (genes!) your body uses to build itself and function. DNA stands for "deoxyribonucleic acid." ✿

molecule: A molecule is the smallest particle of a substance that has all the properties of that substance. For example, one molecule of water looks and behaves like water, but if you broke it down further into its individual parts, it wouldn't be water anymore. Molecules are the basic building blocks for all the substances in our body. DNA, genes, cells, and tissues are all made of molecules. ✿

microscope: A microscope is a tool used to look at things that are too small to see with just our eyes. With a microscope, tiny things look really big! You can use a microscope to look at many things, including the cells that make up your body. ✿

inherited: In science, for something to be inherited it must have been passed down from a parent to a child. You can say that you inherited your brown eyes from your mom if you got the brown version of the eye color gene from her. ✿

trait: A trait is a feature or quality that describes a person. A person can be short, have lots of freckles, and like to eat vegetables—these are all traits. Genes have a big effect on some of your traits, but the world around you also influences your traits. ✿

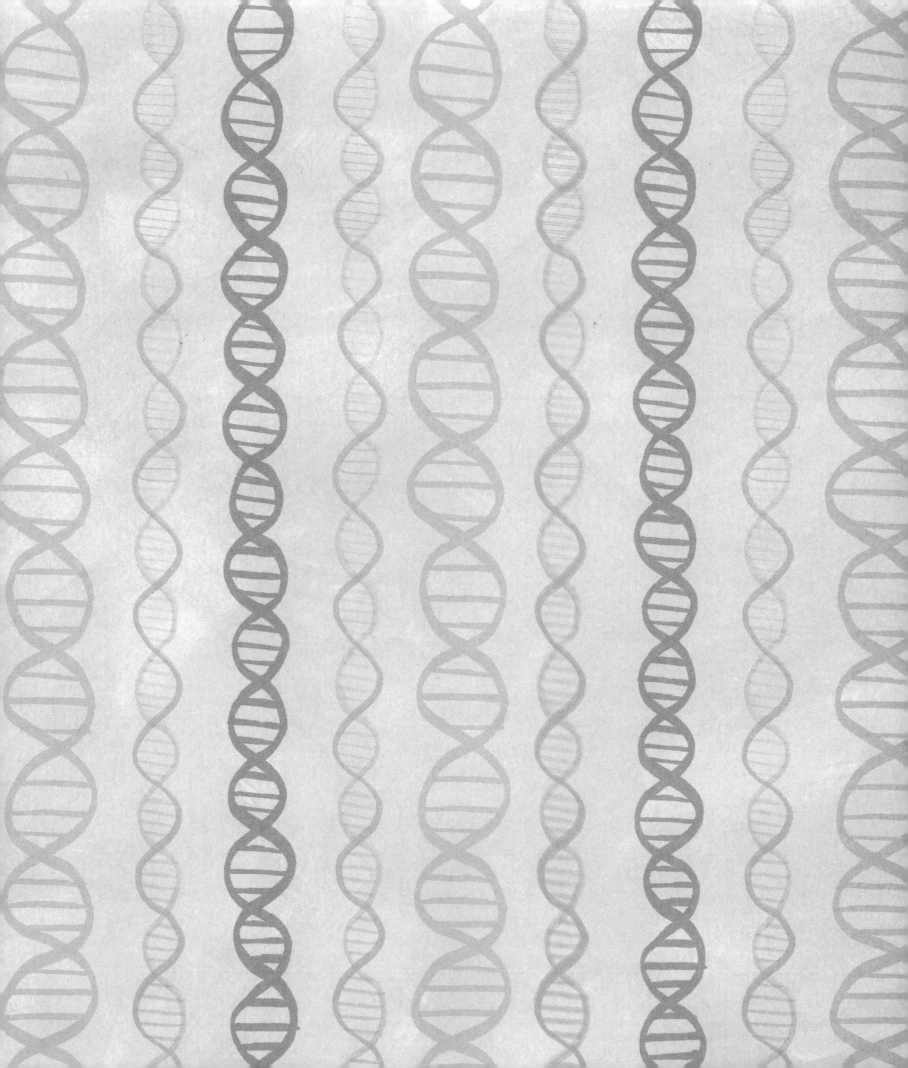

Make-Your-Own Family Tree

There are many ways to make a family tree. Here's a very simple one that can help you guess where some of your physical traits came from.

You will need:

Something to draw WITH.

GRANDPA
(my dad's father)

Paper   cardboard

Something to draw ON.

Family photos.

Step 1:

Draw this tree. Add photos of your parents and grandparents. If you have sisters and brothers, put their photos next to your photo at the bottom of the tree.

Step 2:

Compare and contrast your traits with those you see in your family. From which side of the family might you have gotten your hair color or eye color? Hair texture? Your height? If you have sisters and brothers, from whom do you think they got their traits?